T0195651

Distractions of the Heart

"by Allisha Marie"

authorHOUSE®

AuthorHouse™
1663 Liberty Drive
Bloomington, IN 47403
www.authorhouse.com
Phone: 1 (800) 839-8640

Published by AuthorHouse 07/26/2018

ISBN: 978-1-5462-4966-5 (sc)
ISBN: 978-1-5462-4964-1 (hc)
ISBN: 978-1-5462-4965-8 (e)

Library of Congress Control Number: 2018907834

Print information available on the last page.

Contents

Dedication:

I dedicate this book to my mother for identifying my gift of writing and pushing me to further explore my talent. To my father for always encouraging me to never give up and keep working towards what I want in life. And to my daughter who inspires me to be the best mom I can be along with accepting her mother's relationship choices.

"Anticipating Your Return"

Sitting on this couch as the thoughts
race through my mind.
My behind begins to slouch down.
My hand reaches my inner thigh.
Where this is about to go is going to
Make me feel so high.
As my hand begins to climb
to the waist band of
my pants and tuck.
My mind can only focus on me
wanting to fuck
and possibly make love.
But could I if you're not even near
that when I began to catch the tear
between my legs.
But it kept flowing
as I kept moaning.
And then I thought
before I became distraught.
How could I get you to come back
and finish what I've started.
Long before we departed
and separated during the end of our night.
Damn I wish you'd come back
cause this feels so right.
I hear a knock

And hoping it's you.
Somehow in my mind I thought you knew.
Knew this feeling that I'm experiencing.
But it's not you at the door.
Damn I won't get to experience you anymore.
Tonight that is.
But you'll be back tomorrow
and it's love I will borrow.
For now, I'll just have to finish
and be a menace
and continue to have you in my thoughts,
In my vision.
And I won't forget
To mention my warmth between.
I won't have to tell you
What that means.
Nor will I have to tell you where to go.
Cause that's something
You'll already know.
But let me get off one last time.
Cause if I don't get you off my mind.
Continuing to reach ecstasy,
I could lose track of time.
Cause this feels so real.
Basically this is how you feel.

"Beauties Inner Self"

Looking at the texture of your skin
Some think your not so hot
You're an unwanted person
Just because of the way you look
I think people shouldn't be judged by
the texture of their outer appearance
Be judged on:
how you act
how you treat people
And how you carry yourself
Beauty is with in
And if you feel you can't except
who the person is on the inside
You don't deserve to have that person
as a friend or loved one.
So remember
Beauty comes from within
And if you think otherwise
What beauty does a person like you have?

"Betrayal"

As I'm walking down the street
I feel the drops of rain
continuing to pour down
and moisten my face.
Not realizing that
rain was no more.
The traces of memories
restoring in my mind
The same spoken words
brought forth by others
Will you be my light?
My flower?
My earth?
My everything?
Then that struck of lightening
After romancing
and passionate love making
Will I be their friend?
No longer their lover,
Their soul mate,
Their rhythm in the sky.
The thought of commitment,
Relationship,
Being Locked Down,
has backed their mind
into a corner
that they can't ecscape.

Yet in the vision
that I had was
Fun,
Games,
Sex,
Friendship,
and nothing more.
The assumptions that
has crossed their minds
had made them loss my
Trust,
Respect,
Sexual episodes in bed,
and even my ability to
remain friends with them
because it has left me
to believe in nothing they say
All the lies
and stories they told
left them with one thing
The stress and pain
of self betrayal from realizing
they lost a good woman.

"Brought to Light"

As I walk upon the sun
I see myself
As I look upon the distant sky
I see my light
I look down and beyond
To see the darkness
That has been stored unto me
Starring unto the all mighty
The spirit shall lead me into
The right direction.
The area in which I want to go
Making the decision to embrace a new existence
Changing the life once known by few.
Now being accepted by many.
Seeking the known but unsighted.
Challenging myself to become new.
Feeling the spirit that embraced upon my soul.
Knowing who I want to be.
Knowing why I've changed
His love saved me.
Now feeling fresh and clean
He washed my sins and
Brought me into the Light.

"Caught in Between"

How does it start?
How does it end?
All you know is
Yall started off as friends.
Taking strolls
And going to Super Bowls.
Celebrating each other's birthdays.
Then spend time on holidays.
Going to the store buying candy.
Then sitting up all night listening to Brandy.
Watching each other's relationships rot.
But yall still manage to recite poetry for each other
At the five spot.
Looking at a woman who's a potential hottie.
But in the back of your mind
You want to explore
Your best friend's body.
The more time yall spend together.
The more you want her forever.
While your living arrangements are falling apart.
It's her you wanted as your heart.
Your boy had her as his girl.
But in reality, you wanted to explore her world.
You want her so bad.
But you have to remember now you're a "dad".
With her you know you won't go through major drama.
Compared to the one you're going through with your "baby mama".
Trying to work it out with one.
But wanting her to have your son.
Her mind and body you've seen.
But your still caught in between.

"Consequence By Another"

Someone who enters the realm of fire
expects their flesh to melt away,
their blood to boil along with
the moisture in the air, and
their bones to shed as ashes
as they fall into the dirty clouds of gases.
Someone who takes a stroll in the park
near a dark alley at night
suspects someone is lurking near
and is wanting to violate one's temple
that has been kept clean
through the practice of abstinence and
2nd born again virginity.
Someone who admires another from afar
expects to draw attention of such beauty
and gravitates toward this lonely soul
only to find their spirit and mentality
is connected to another
causing one to feel rejection and humiliation.
Someone who takes their heart
and places it in front of another,
who has rejected what the meaning
of a heart signifies and has thrown
hatred back into one's universe,
stating love is not supplied and
friendship is not the answer,

has suffered from a loss
that has deteriorated one's inner flow of energy,
one's thinking process,
and one's breathing of the air
that once smelled so fresh
and so exuberant.
However, these are the consequences faced
when entering situations
that seem comfortable and lavishing.
Yet deceiving and untamable, when placed
In an unfamiliar surrounding.

"Could It Be"?

My body exploded in my mind
From your fingertips penetrating my skin
reaching under the muscles and blood
creating a sensation to the pumping vessel called my heart.
Your lips got my body dancing on the sun.
Warm vibrations, perspiring from the glide of your tongue.
The rhythmic and intense pressure
causing pulsing sensations
while the moisture escapes and flows beyond the ocean floors.
It is You!
The pleasure in my dream finally standing next to me
enhancing my intellect
through the educational tones of your voice.
It has to be You!
The only replica of my display
where affection and affirmation intertwine
leaving me locked into your transitional stare of lust, desire, love.
I need it to be You!
In the absence of your presence,
my obsession intensifies
pondering on the mental optics of your silhouette.
Thought provoking to lead my warmth and
pleasurable hands to converse.
I want it to be You!
The level of trouble you possess
shatters my preconceived views of what I expected,
I needed,

and allowing for patience to reside in my
tears allowing for our connectional growth.
Could it be You?
Signs displayed where entrapment
of each step taken is reserved
for painting a new journey designed for us by you.
Meanwhile, your positional stance
has been implanted yet gone unnoticed.
Somewhere time changed,
head lifted,
and your soul met mine.
So yes, it's You!

"Destiny Of Love"

Expanding thoughts
Threw the mind.
The force stopping the force.
While it's in a train of thought.
Stealing the precious minutes in time.
Exchange of private numerals.
Now.
What is it?
Force wanting to imply destiny.
Thinking other wise.
But now,
Can it be the destination
One's seeking.
Forming the letters
of one's feelings.
Importing three special words.
Can it be true.
Has true love come my way.
For you,
The one called destiny.
It is true.
Emotions hit me
with the touch of happiness.
In coming,
What I never thought would be.
Could it be.
Should it be.
My thoughts tell me

to escape from one's sight.
But,
My heart tells me
to expand on what is found.
Explore it.
See it.
Feel it.
Touch it.
Smell it.
Reach out to it.
Oh, one doesn't know how to react.
This can be true.
My inner self tells me
I have explored special feelings.
Feelings I never knew exist.
Until that soul mate was found.
Speaking words,
never thought twice about expressing.
But now,
Feeling as if the spiritual giver
is my soul mate,
my destiny.
I spoke those three words.

"Distractions of the Heart"

Not sure why all these distractions occur.
It started off with the sound from the phone's ring,
Putting a slight pause in my breath
Causing me to rush towards it
Only to realize it's someone else.
Why the desperation in my walk?
Leaving out the door
and noticing a similar car drive by
with the same tinted windows
pulling over to park and I smile
only to hinder the steps in my strides
and a shadow of disappointment lay upon my lips
as I reiterate out loud,
Why would I ever think you would just show up?
Taking a break at work
and observing a gift set of flowers
and edible arrangements be delivered
and remembering your text earlier
stating you had a surprise coming to my job
all while the surprise never showed.
Why do I continue to believe the lies?
Deciding to move on to someone new
only to begin to receive the recognition,
gifts, affection, and affirmation promised from you.
Why does the little things from you still make me smile?
Just when I emphasize
the need to start over with this someone new,
you utter and demonstrate more consistently

the word and action called "LOVE".
Why do I continue to believe what you say?
It's these simple distractions
that open the flood gates to my cries,
the pain behind my heart,
the constant wandering if I'm enough.
All while questioning
if you've really changed,
if your ready to be what I need.
End result being
inconsistency,
deception,
confusion,
and exonerating self from commitment.
Why the juggling of emotions and actions on your end?
It's plain and clear
that you distracted my heart
to avoid others from having
what you can't seem to want yourself.
My Heart!

"Final Confession"

Ok so I guess it's going to have to be me that makes this call
After all you don't know how bad you mad me fall
That is become deep within thought, mesmerized by your touch
Not knowing that I miss you so much
But what should I say
Should it be I miss you, want you, need you, or
Let's get away for the day
Maybe all the above
Cause as I sit back and think
Damn have I really fallen in love?
That can't be possible nor can it be true
It's only been a few...
That is a few stolen moments
Where we've spent time and space
How I would give any given moment just to see your face.
Therefore it's time for me to be a woman
And say what I want
And not continue to put up this front
So here I go as I dial the numbers on this phone...
what the hell the voicemail
You mean to tell me she not even home.
Ok no need to panic we'll just leave a message
And it'll go like this,
"Babe' I miss you and want us to be one,
I miss your laugh, I miss all the fun,
I know I played a part in messing things up,

So can we get over this and just make up,
I'll hold you close, I'll hold you tight,
Shit I'll even cook for you in the middle of the night,
I'll do it all, I'll aim to please
I'm gonna show you it's me that can satisfy and provide all your needs
So hurry and call me back
And FYI I got on that teddy you like in blue and black"
I must say that was a good message to leave
Now let's see if she calls back and actually believes.....

"For my love"

Glancing at the sky.
Deciding to sit and watch
the sunrise.
While falling into
each other's eyes.
It may have come to
no surprise
when you laid me down
next to your side.
Placing my face in your chest
as if burying it to hide.
The warmth of your touch.
Oh how I've grown
to love you so much.
The sensation of your kiss.
Hopefully something I would
never have to miss.
When you stop to look
and caress my face,
I no longer wonder about
someone ever taking my place.
You've given me a taste
of your style and grace
to show me what you're about.
And never leaving me
with any doubt,
about where I stand.

And if I do,
you take my hand
to try and make
me understand
the truth of it all.
Realizing it was you
who called,
me everyday
just to say
you care,
to share,
and be there,
for my love.

"Girls, Ladies, & Women"

You come and you yell.
You break and you bail.
Bail on misery and pain
That has built within.
Now there's neither
A smile or a grin.
There's no trust in your heart
Or a sense of self-worth.
But you worry about
Where the next guy or girl is coming from
And how much they are worth.
What about what's in your pocket.
And what's in your brain.
It's not about what someone else can do for you,
It's how much you gain.
Gain from experience
And from knowledge.
How many of you actually thought about college?
No one can steal your joy
And steal your pride.
No matter how much anger, pain, confusion has derived.
You step out of that box
Into open space.
Learning self-worth, patience,
anger management, style and grace.
I guarantee not even you
will be able to go back in time

And dwell on being lonely,
Suffering from insanity,
Or not having a single dime.
Making that effort
To break down that wall,
It's either you rise
Or either you fall.
In order to blossom into a rose
Or a beautiful flower.
That wall must become your desire.
Desire to succeed in life.
But first you must get rid of
That negativity, fear, and strife.
Build on the here and now.
Instead of your hopes and dreams
Shattering to the ground.
For now pick up that frown.
Walk around with your crown.
Don't allow yourself to drown.
It's in you to take heed
Of your own destiny.
So no one will take over the
Best of Thee.

"Hurt to Healing"

While sleeping through the night
Pondering on issues that no one could imagine
Issues that keep my eyes wide open
in the middle of the night.
Being frightened to continue through dreams of terror.
Trying to escape the harsh realities
of what is going on.
Nothing so horrible has ever happened to me
Why now?
Why this?
Why me?
No one should know.
No one can know.
What should I do?
I'm ashamed of me
Who I have become.
What I participated in.
My feelings could no longer be the same.
Was I at the wrong place at the wrong time.
Was I at the right place at the right time.
Was this meant to happen.
I'll hide it.
No one shall know.
It will be my secret.
I've become a new person.
But with the same feelings.
Nothing can harm me now.

I am untouchable.
No one or Nothing
will ever hurt me.
I'm going for mine.
I've decided to start over.
Think about me first.
Find out what's best for me.
It's time for me to shine.
It's time for me to get mine.
I need to get my priorities straight.
Then when it's time.
I'll communicate again.
I'll be a changed women.
A better person
One who will make the right decision.
Decisions on life, and relationships.

"Lack of Appreciation"

Who cares what you say
As I turned around
And walked away.
Not listening to the negativity
There is no sensitivity
Left in my heart.
Cause from the start
You never wanted to see me succeed.
But so far,
I've proved you wrong indeed.
You have no love
For those who achieve on their own.
But you refused
To leave me alone.

Why is it so hard
To say its over?
Why is it so hard
To say goodbye?
Why is it so hard
To make up your mind?

Its hard because
There are still things
That you still deny.
Whether you still love me
Cherish me,

And accept me.
For who I want to be.
But you can't bare
To see
Nor commend me
For doing the things
You wanted to do.
Because I've achieved more
You still punish me for
Being independent,
Devoted,
And dedicated.
When it should be you
To blame
For being uneducated.
Why is it so hard
To say its over?
Why is it so hard
To say goodbye?
Why is it so hard
To make up your mind?

Till this day
You say
You didn't know
If you fell in love
With my mind, body, or soul.
Once I started to show you
I had total control

Of my decisions,
My life with you,
In your eyes,
Started to be questionable.
Then you gave the excuse
Of it not being you.
And that it was I
Who wasn't being reasonable.
So for this
I had to leave
And now
You call and grieve.
About missing my touch
My love,
My conversation.
But its too late
Because I've moved on
To someone with appreciation.

"Lifes Questions"

What does it mean
When someone
looks into your eyes?
Does it mean they adore you?
Does it mean they want you?
Or does it mean they want to kiss you?
What does it mean
When someone holds your hand?
Do they enjoy your company?
So they want everyone to know your theirs?
Or do they enjoy the sensation of a gentle touch?
What does it mean
When someone doesn't return your call?
So they no longer cherish you?
So they no longer feel the need to keep in contact?
Or do they have another in your place?
What does it mean
When someone breaks your heart?
From experience,
It means your left with pain.
It means you're stuck with sorrow.
It means you're filled with grief.
It means you're sad and blue.
It means you're mad at the world.
It means you can no longer trust.
It means you cry
till there are no more tears.
Out of all questions
Why is this the easiest to answer?

"Lonely Soul"

Traveling to a great distance
While in a deep train of thought
Thinking of the possibilities
and the uncertainty
of one's commitment.
The choice remains unknown.
Randomly choosing the right suspect.
No, Selecting the opposite of inner self.
The intake of emotional distress.
Why pursue the impossible?
The heartless sound one hears.
The soul that disappears into the night.
Revealing itself time and time again.
In long waiting periods.
Expanding seconds into minutes,
minutes into hours, hours into days,
Perhaps days into weeks.
Why continue to praise the unknown?
Sounds once heard
but for a sudden moment
that sound is silenced.
Forcing sound to reappear.
Why initiate continuous pain upon one's self?
Blinded by the love
Which one's holding inside.
Falling too deep
Caring too much

Making an effort to benefit
not two, maybe only one.
One must come and explore.
Coming to conclusions with reality.
Finding no one around
No one to care,
No one to hold,
No one to touch,
Or no one in the presence
to see a lonely soul.

"Mentally Orgasmic"

Your words hit me over the head
And hauled me into a daze.
As you fumble over words
And articulate them into a sensual meaning.
My mental capacity begins to form your words in a daydream.
Who would have known letters could be pieced together
to reiterate one's inner sensitivities toward another.
Then sanctioning words of wisdom
to carry over into the heightened conversation,
Conveying forth stimulation so great
that it collapses your process of any sexual stimulation
amongst the body and captures every spoken word
then freezes it after every single phrase
causing the consciousness to spasm
and reverberate
and wail
and move the way my body would
if it was licked
and made loved to
in order to perform an orgasmic experience.
But see,
when words are scattered around
and the temple of one's persona
is craving this type of dialect,
the mind ruptures
like a volcanic ash eruption
trying to apprehend the meaning of
this mentally orgasmic sensation.
However, this moment is so vast
it conquers a real sexual explosive episode.

"Moist"

Dripping and stepping over the top.
Lifting that leg over that porcelain white.
She knows it's late,
But when she gets out that shower,
she plans to be fresh bate.
For now she will enjoy the steam,
as she leans along the shower wall.
Truly her name she calls,
as the suds run down her breast,
and then her hands begin to caress.
Only a place where she wants her to touch,
and taste,
and make her body feel graceful and loved.
Well tonight she don't want no damn hugs.
She wants to feel her deep inside.
So deep enough for her to cry,
And scream,
And quiver.
Only her name will shiver through her body
And sounds of her voice she will hear.
Damn she says,
As she's not even out the shower,
And already
She's moist…

"My Love For Ever"

When we set out on this journey.
A few things for me weren't true.
I thought I'd never find love.
But then I was drawn to you.
I expected to be afraid of
Every move I made
And continue to wonder
If things for me would ever change.
Then you rearranged my world
And allowed me to be free and feel safe.
You blocked all my thoughts of worry
And placed in my path,
A new sense of direction.
One that will hide
My shadows of pain
And commence the smile
That you placed upon my heart and soul.
I never presented the notion of
Wanting to commit my time and energy
Into focusing on another,
In order to learn and appreciate them.
With you,
Getting to study every move,
Every breath,
Every emotion within
Your body movement
And facial expressions,
Gives me glory and honor
To know I can put forth more time learning you.

I never thought
I would know what LOVE felt like.
That was until you came
And paid attention,
Embraced me with your warmth,
Placed me in your arms,
And assured my world
You would make alright.
I didn't want to kiss anyone else's lips.
That was until,
Your lips touched mine,
My eyes became blind
From your single kiss
And made the words
I wanted to express become speechless.
Who knew a single person could
Make you change your ways
And feel complete.
Because of this new insight on LOVE,
I want to cherish you for ever.
And make you my wife.
Now that is a thought,
That just didn't exist.
You must truly be my love
That was brought forth by a wish.

"Nothing Lasts Forever!"

Why can't I seem to get it together?
Surely nothing lasts forever!
The rope was tied so tight.
However, the knots got loose
And no longer were you in sight.
Somehow, I thought that day would come
Where those memories would be erased
And those regrets I would no longer taste.
But now it seems so clear.
That you're neither far or near.
But in reach
Enough to grab my hand.
And perhaps take a stand.
That stand called lasting friendship
Which I'll cherish
But fear.
Cause my love for you
Is neither far or near.
But in the middle
And that's ok.
Cause nothing ever lasts anyway.
Right!!!!

"Realization"

Eye to eye connection
drew me into your world.
Your way of embracing me
heighten my level of comfort.
The way you cuddle and
wrap your body around mine
builds trust and sense of need.
Prepping and preparing a meal
in such delicacy shows
determination and care for
keeping up my well-being.
Gracefully removing my shoes
after a long day of work
shows concern for my
mental stability and an urgency
For wanting to be closer.
Placing my hand in yours
just to transfer the love
within your heart.
Seems all these things are
unreal and easily transferable.
And as I open my eyes
and realize all that is
only remains true actions of my own.
it's only my thoughts, dreams, and
wishes that's only returned.
Realization of it is,
more doesn't exist.

"Sensually Known"

Where does one find the unknown?
When something or someone
Is so mysterious,
One takes a step back
And admires beauty and prestige.
When that beauty is sensual
And touches every being of one's soul.
And erases every thought in the unconscious.
Then caresses your body with words.
The energy that flows from the finger tips
Sets one's body on fire and
Lifts up the emotions that has been
Hidden deep down and underneath
The surface of the skin and tissues of the bones.
At the point where the unknown has been
The known and
The one who sets comfort
And soothes the essence
Of a gentle touch in order to
Guide the arch of one's foot
With the curve of one's spin.
When the unknown is brought
Forth to the light and
Addresses the issue of connecting
The psyche with a body that
Has never been controlled and
Conquered, one begins to

Understand the nature of the two
Bodies being joined in harmony.
But harmony controls the rhythm
And smooths out the vibrations
That allows these two bodies to
Finally connect and share
A sensual and sexual moment
That brings the universe and
The star to a standstill.
But the Earth is still moving
Forcing gravity to pull the unknown
Towards a body which has been
Waiting to be explored.
Now that the unknown has experienced,
Conquered, and drawn its energy
And placed it within the one who
Has been waiting,
Love and Faith
Symbolizes the new existence
Of what was already sensually known.

"Sex, Love, & Pain"

Capture each moment
In the presence that it's given
In the beginning of the process.
Sex.
The touching of two souls.
The connection of heated attraction.
Throwing out the possibility of
Even being connected physically,
Mentally, and spiritually.
Sex being the only factor.
Until later on
The fire getting stronger,
The water running softer,
The cupids' arrow has struck.
Love.
Entering the picture which
Has already been drawn
Attempting to resist temptation
Getting caught up in the game.
Letting passion and intimacy occur
Love fills the heart again.
And as usual the killer of all time.
Pain.
Realizing what could never be.
Causing sex and love
To take over the mind and body

Which is now corrupted
By the pain and misery
Of trying to be with.
In this game
You have to pick and choose.
Sex or Love.
If you continue to let it,
The body takes over the mind and soul.
You will be left with
Sex, Love, & Pain.

"Shopping Cart"

Most often during the rain
this young girl felt pain
and rage in her heart
as all her emotions built up in a shopping cart.
And each time, she went to put something back.
More fear piled up in stacks.
She couldn't figure out how these things came about.
But she took a look and pulled some out.
Then again somethings were left behind.
Like the rape, molestation, and abuse
That reflected in her mind.
At that moment she realized her frustrations,
anger, and hostility was built on top of things.
But they all were attached to each other
and stuck to the bottom of this cart.
Somehow this continued
to leave a hole in her heart.
Her desire to put these things
back on the shelf
would only rebuild her wealth
And desire to live.
For she, at one point in life
no longer wanted to cry
as she recollected on that moment
she wanted to die.
So she reached into that cart
only to rebuild

her heart, mind, soul, and flesh.
Each item put back
would depreciate as she said
"I don't need this".
Noticing her price for life was higher in cost
and she could live in eternal bliss.
But it took her to go shopping
to see all the things placed in her cart.
But now she has new items
and is ready for a new start.

"Shoulder 2 Cry On"

As the night rolls around,
I lay in bed thinking of you.
Trying to get you out of my mind.
Trapped by the thoughts and memories
we once shared.
Having you there to grasp
every feeling and emotion
just from a single word spoken.
The only one who could
deal with all my pain within.
You were my strength, my guidance,
my friend, and my lover.
Giving me the opportunity to release.
Lending me your shoulder 2 cry on.
Helped me get in touch with
the pain I was struggling with.
But tell me this.
After all the pain I went through
in lovin you.
Who will be my shoulder 2 cry on now?

"Silent Words"

Most people don't understand
Why I keep to myself.
They neglect to see
the pain in my eyes,
the look on my face.
Even the stride in my walk
has no words
that can be expressed.
The vibrations of my voice
when I speak
is a give away but,
some don't take the time
to listen to my story.
So trying to avoid
the stress of explaining
how I feel inside,
I keep to myself.
Late at night
when siting in my room
in the darkness,
I sit and think
and try to expand my mind
on issues that has never been solved.
Releasing my feelings and my inner pain
Through sobs and tears.
Wondering why I'm not loved
and made to feel beautiful.

Wanting to know why
I'm not appreciated
but, taken advantage of.
There's not one person
who can understand
My pain,
My mind,
My inner soul,
My stride in my walk,
My tone in my voice,
My broken heart,
My expressions on my face,
My touch from my fingers
And especially,
The look in my eyes.
But no one will ever know
Why I keep my
Words Silent.

"Someone Special"

Searching in the mist of sorrow.
Trying to fulfill one's destiny.
Needing that warmth of comfort.
Never reaching that destination.
That is until now.
Finally noticing what has been there all along.
A provider,
who will ease the pain within
by comforting my mind.
A receiver,
who will take in my love and
recycle it to warmth their own soul.
A friend,
who will not only be there to
advise me on how to stay strong
During my struggles, but also
be there to console me when I'm down.
A lover,
who will satisfy my body with their
touch and my mind with their words.
A fighter,
who will strive to any distance to
keep something precious and special together
to make a relationship work.
And hopefully
My soulmate,
One that I am destined to be with,

to fall in love with,
and never desire or want
to be with another soul.
Because the one presented
before me hopefully will be here
until the end of our days.
Finally finding all these qualities
in one who was almost over looked.
It would have been a lost.
And my journey for love
would have continued.
And my life as I know it
would still be a disaster
and Incomplete.

"Thank You For Saving My Spirit"

Hiding from the outside world
Keeping to my soul
Feeling empty and dirty
Remembering the feeling of an unwanted touch
Not wanting to confide in anyone
People closest to my soul not knowing how I'm feeling
Waking up every night
Sweating from the nightmare of that unwanted touch
My spirit crying itself to sleep night after night
No one can seem to get close anymore
Shutting everyone out
Except now, I've found someone I can trust
Someone I can get close too
You erased all the sadness away
Escaping from the world is something I still do
But I'm starting to come out of my shell
Thank you for saving me from my fears of the outside world
And for that
I thank you
Thank you for saving
My mind and soul.

"The Essence of Touch"

As I sit here and gaze at a closed window shade,
I can't help but to recapture the essence of your scent.
My mind drifting to the various colors you left on my heart.
The consonants and vows you spoke to electrify my mind
bringing forth repeated regurgitating episodes of self-touch.
Slow breaths due to gasping from the piercing of your lips puncturing
my skin.
Visioning the moments of your glance reaching
the locked gates of my soul
and watching your presence make it open.
Wondering if your mind escapes in remembrance
of rotating moments of pleasure
allowing sounds beyond gravitational pull.
Passing the shade to open the window
cause I'm suffocating in thought of the essence of your touch.
The breeze entering then seeping through my pours
like orgasmic vibrations you placed on my mind
from your fingertips gliding the place where my thoughts reside.
It was something about the intertwining and locking of our hands
replicating the affection of your tongue
unlocking my inner frustration.
My body moistens to the hold of your grasp
against the curves in my hour glass
while penetrating the shell that's been fighting you off.
But how can I run?
How can I hide?
When your nose is pressed against my temple

making its way to my neck
pulling out moments of silence and fragments of fainting spells.
Becoming light on my feet
from the strength of your biceps
having my structure pulled close
releasing the sounds of high pitch tones.
Exhaling silent breaths
thanks to the tone of my name released off the tip of your tongue.
Why does this woman feel so right?
Only the elements of her
can surpass an intimate level that quivers
even the sound of my moans and weakening of my limbs.
But it's the essence of her touch
that can reach my subconscious thoughts
replicating orgasmic mental stimulation
desiring more than a sexual encounter
but requiring her affection.

"The Sit Of Silence"

Sitting under a brisk of leaves
looking up into the darkness of night
staring into the brightness of diamonds
listening to the sounds of silence
Only to wash out the misery inside of me
The emptiness inside of me
Is tearing me apart
from my real innermost secrets
What are those innermost secrets?
What shall I learn from them?
What can I acknowledge from it?
Only one person can tell me
What I am feeling inside
Is it because I'm weak
Is it because I'm strong
Or is it because I'm a woman
looking for her own?
The only thing I can see
Is that there's only one secret inside of me
The secret to strive for:
my dreams
my goals
my thirst for knowledge
and to help every man and woman in trouble
Is this why I sit here straining my brain?
If so, then it was worth it?
because I've found out
I'm more than the woman I contemplated to be!

"The Storm & The Sky"

A night of misery.
A night of pain.
Here comes the mourning
with a splash of rain.
Spread across a soft layer of silk & satin.
Trying to figure out what will happen.
The blinds begin to close.
Here comes mourning,
What will occur nobody knows.
Dirty clouds in the sky.
Fog begins to cover why?
Outside yelling it's ok.
Maybe bad weather,
But I won't face you anymore today.
I'd rather have a brighter day.
Then to let this weather take my joy away.
Seeing that I was right
In the sky I saw something bright.
The clouds begin to move
And the sun begins to rise.
Causing the storm to fall by its side.
Coming forth.
In bringing warmth.
Spraying rays
On the stormy days.
What brings the warm weather here.
Was it my past.

Or was it the fear.
Having to face up to the thunder & lightening.
But the sun,
It brought bravery and courage.
So the storm
Could wash away
Along with its current.
But who's to say
The storm won't reappear.
But in faith,
I don't think so
as long as the sun stays risen here.
Here in the sky resembling my life.

Printed in the United States
By Bookmasters